EASY GUITAR
WITH NOTES & TAB

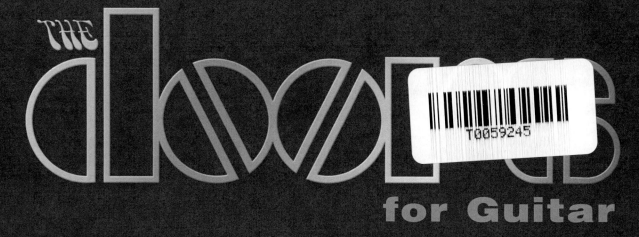

for Guitar

Cover photography by Henry Diltz

ISBN 0-634-00215-5

HAL•LEONARD®
CORPORATION
7777 W. BLUEMOUND RD. P.O. BOX 13819 MILWAUKEE, WI 53213

Visit Hal Leonard Online at
www.halleonard.com

THE dOOrs

Contents

STRUM AND PICK PATTERNS

This chart contains the suggested strum and pick patterns that are referred to by number at the beginning of each song in this book. The symbols ⊓ and ∨ in the strum patterns refer to down and up strokes, respectively. The letters in the pick patterns indicate which right-hand fingers plays which strings.

p = thumb
i = index finger
m = middle finger
a = ring finger

For example; Pick Pattern 2
is played: thumb - index - middle - ring

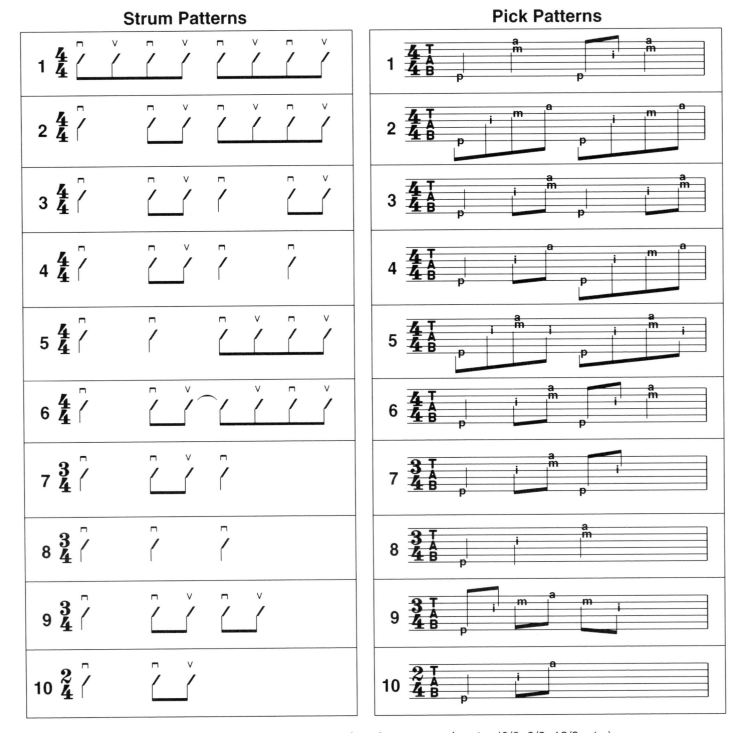

You can use the 3/4 Strum or Pick Patterns in songs written in compound meter (6/8, 9/8, 12/8, etc.).
For example, you can accompany a song in 6/8 by playing the 3/4 pattern twice in each measure.
The 4/4 Strum and Pick Patterns can be used for songs written in cut time (¢) by doubling the note time values in the patterns. Each pattern would therefore last two measures in cut time.

Five to One

Words and Music by The Doors

Strum Pattern: 1, 3
Pick Pattern: 1, 3

Verse
Moderately Fast

1. Five to one, __ ba - by, one in five. __ No one here __ gets

out a - live __ now. __ You get yours, _ ba - by, I'll get mine. __

Gon - na make it, ba - by, if we try. __ The

Chorus

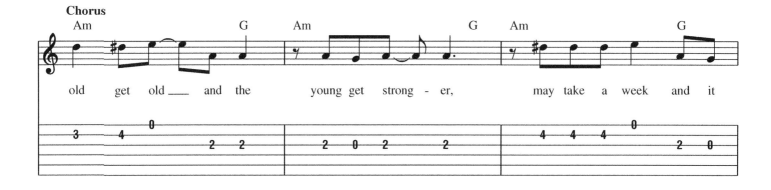

old get old ___ and the young get strong - er, may take a week and it

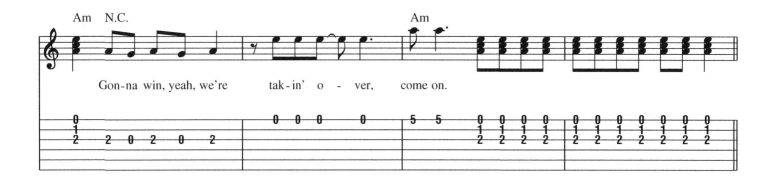

may take long - er. They got the guns but we got the num - bers.

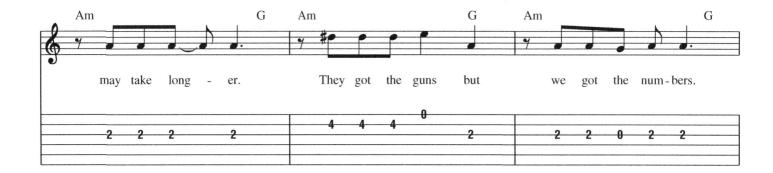

Gon-na win, yeah, we're tak-in' o - ver, come on.

Verse

2. Your ball - room days are o - ver, ba - by, night is draw - ing near.

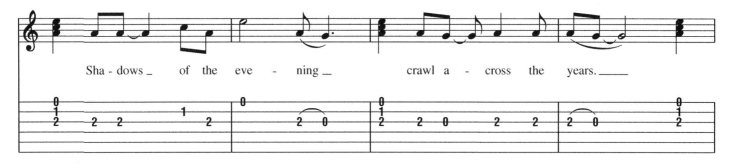

Sha - dows ___ of the eve - ning ___ crawl a - cross the years. ___

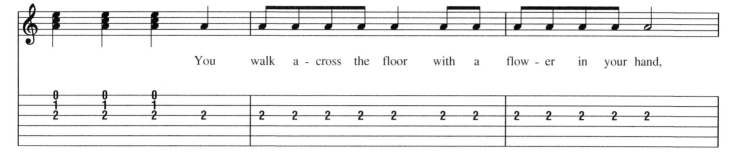

You walk a - cross the floor with a flow - er in your hand,

try - ing to tell me no one un - der - stands. Trade in your hours ___ for a

hand - ful of dimes. ___ Gon - na make it, ba - by, in our prime. _

Outro
Am

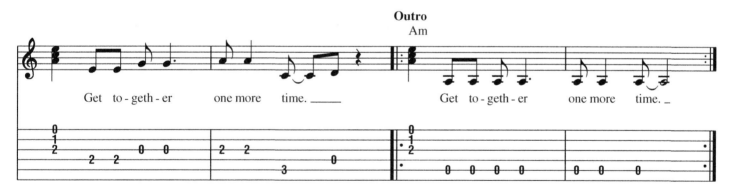

Get to - geth - er one more time. _____ Get to - geth - er one more time. _

Repeat and Fade
Am   G   Am   G

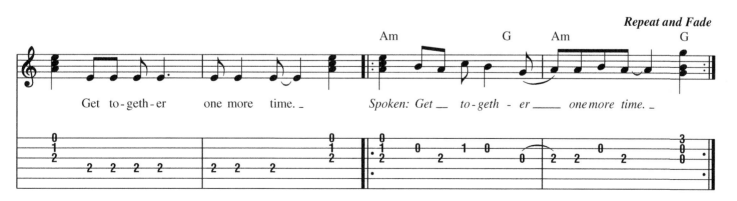

Get to - geth - er one more time. _ *Spoken: Get _ to - geth - er ____ one more time. _*

Break on Through
(To the Other Side)

Words and Music by The Doors

Strum Pattern: 5, 6
Pick Pattern: 5, 6

Intro

Moderately Fast Rock

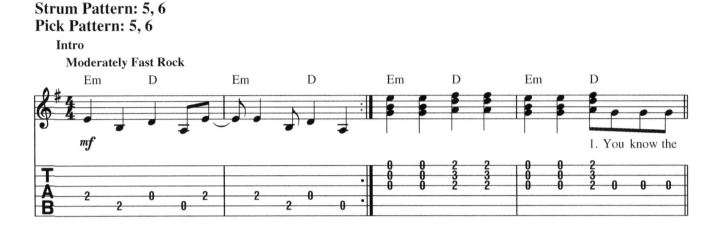

1. You know the

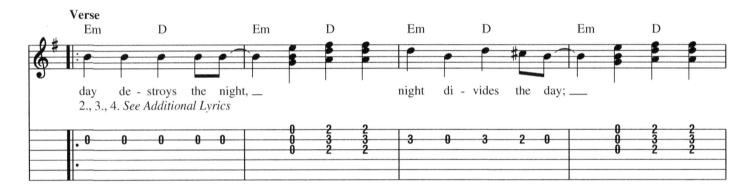

day de-stroys the night, __ night di-vides the day; __

2., 3., 4. See Additional Lyrics

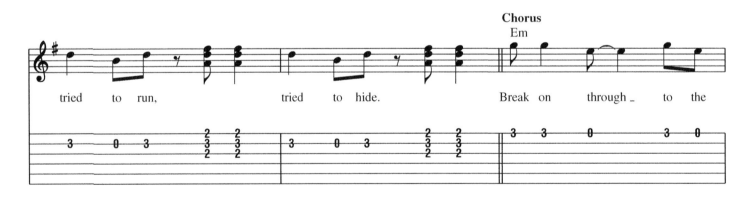

tried to run, tried to hide. Break on through __ to the

oth-er side. __ Break on through __ to the oth-er side. __

Break on through _ to the oth - er side. _ 2. We oth - er side. _

Interlude

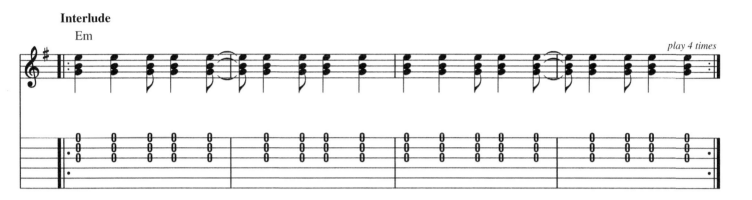

Outro

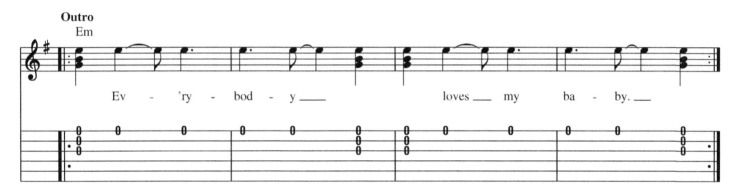

Ev - 'ry - bod - y ___ loves ___ my ba - by. _

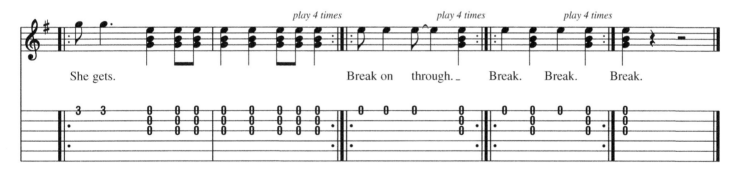

She gets. Break on through. _ Break. Break. Break.

Additional Lyrics

2. We chased our pleasures here,
   Dug our treasures there.
   But can you still recall the time we cried?

3. I found an island in your arms,
   A country in your eyes.
   Arms that chain, eyes that lie.

4. Made the scene from week to week,
   Day to day, hour to hour.
   The gate is straight, deep and wide.

Crystal Ship

Words and Music by The Doors

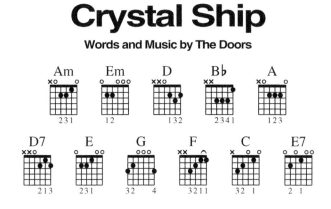

Strum Pattern: 3, 6
Pick Pattern: 3, 6

Moderately Slow

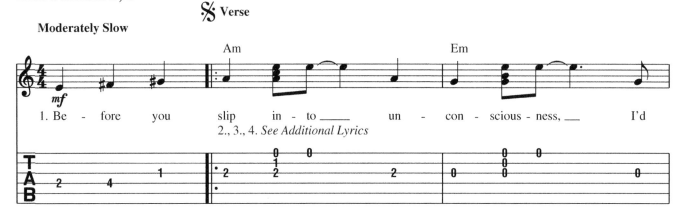

1. Be - fore you slip in - to ___ un - con - scious - ness, ___ I'd
2., 3., 4. *See Additional Lyrics*

like to have an - oth - er kiss, __ an - oth - er flash - ing

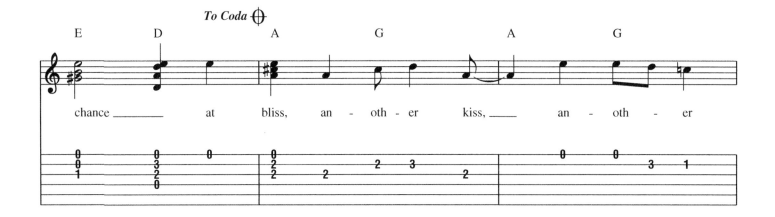

chance _____ at bliss, an - oth - er kiss, ___ an - oth - er

3rd time, D.S. al Coda

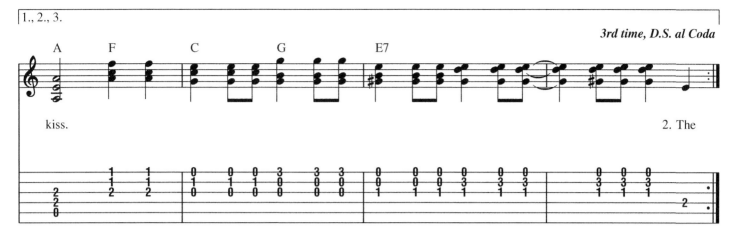

kiss.

2. The

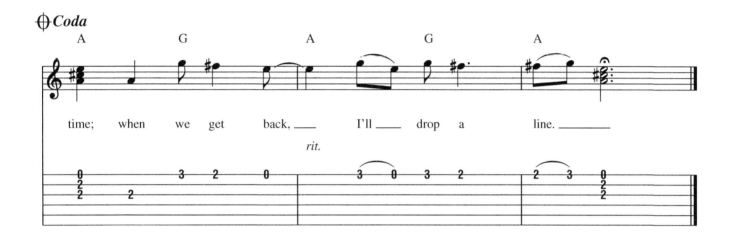

Additional Lyrics

2. The days are bright and filled with pain.
   Enclose me in your gentle rain.
   The time you ran was too insane,
   We'll meet again, we'll meet again.

3. Oh, tell me where your freedom lies,
   The streets are fields that never die.
   Deliver me from reasons why
   You'd rather cry, I'd rather fly.

4. The crystal ship is being filled,
   A thousand girls, a thousand thrills.
   A million ways to spend your time;
   When we get back, I'll drop a line.

End of the Night

Words and Music by The Doors

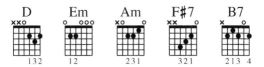

Strum Pattern: 1, 4
Pick Pattern: 1, 5

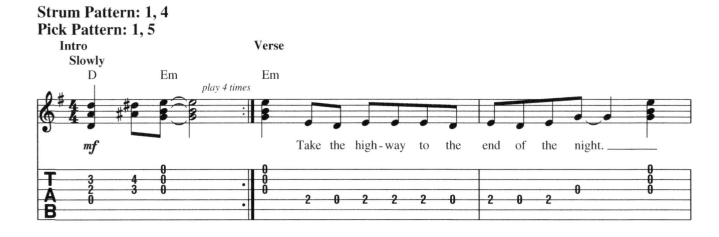

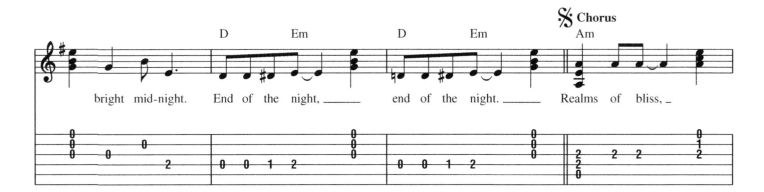

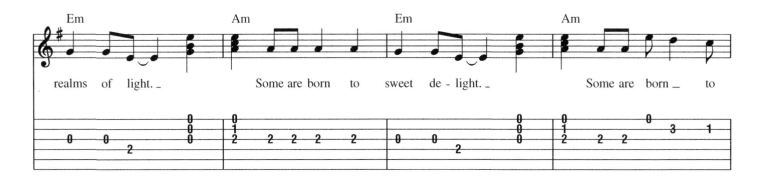

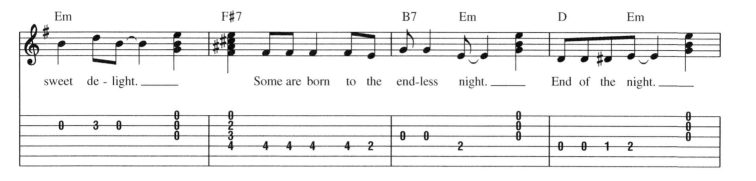

sweet de - light. _____   Some are born   to the   end-less   night. _____   End of the night. _____

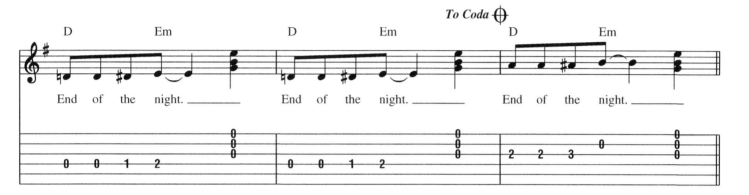

To Coda

End   of   the   night. _____   End   of   the   night. _____   End   of   the   night. _____

Interlude

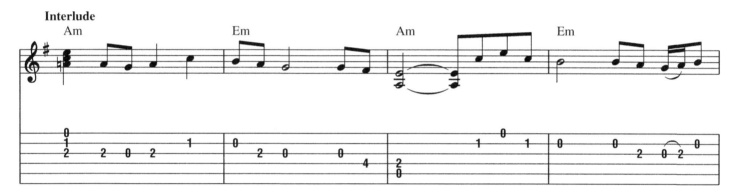

2nd time, D.S. al Coda   ⊕ *Coda*

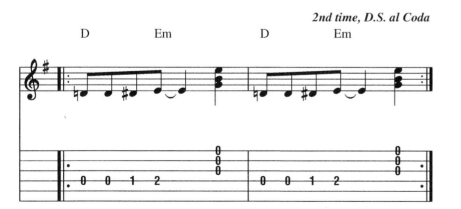

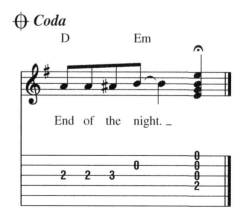

End of the night. _

Hello, I Love You
(Won't You Tell Me Your Name?)

Words and Music by The Doors

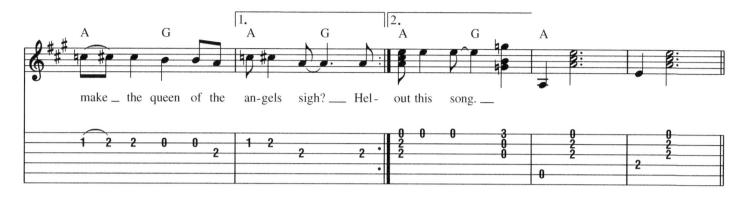

make _ the queen of the an-gels sigh? _ Hel- out this song. _

Bridge

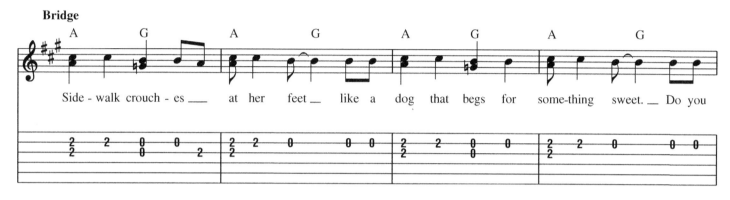

Side - walk crouch - es _ at her feet _ like a dog that begs for some-thing sweet. _ Do you

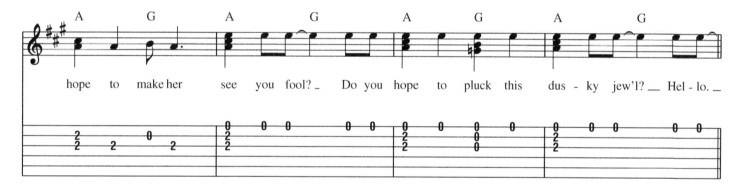

hope to make her see you fool? _ Do you hope to pluck this dus - ky jew'l? _ Hel - lo. _

Outro   *Repeat and Fade*

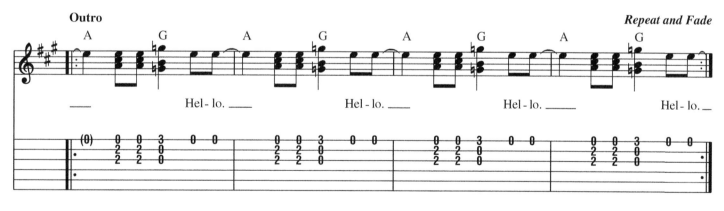

_ Hel - lo. _   Hel - lo. _   Hel - lo. _   Hel - lo. _

Additional Lyrics

2. She holds her head so high,
   Like a statue in the sky.
   Her arms are wicked and her legs are long.
   When she moves, my brain screams out this song.

I Looked at You

Words and Music by The Doors

Strum Pattern: 3, 5
Pick Pattern: 2, 3

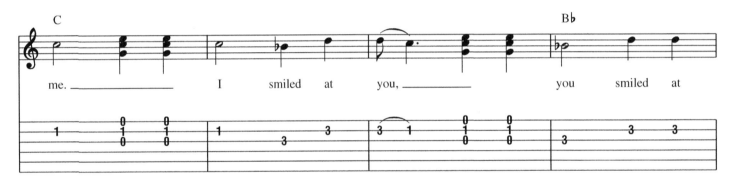

1. I looked at you, _____ you looked at
2. *See Additional Lyrics*

me. _____ I smiled at you, _____ you smiled at

me. And we're on our way, _____ no, we can't turn back, babe.

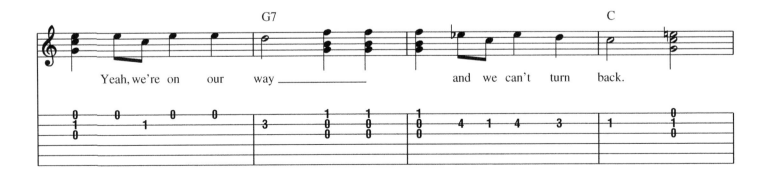

Yeah, we're on our way _____ and we can't turn back.

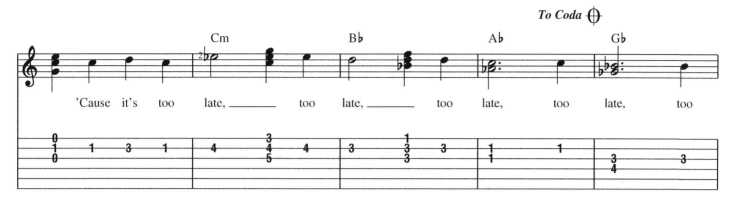

'Cause it's too late, _____ too late, _____ too late, too late, too

late. _____ And we're on our way, no, we can't turn

back, babe. Yeah, we're on our way and we can't turn

D.S. al Coda

⊕ *Coda*

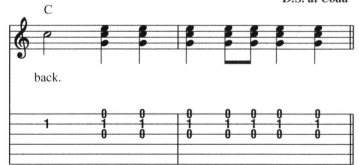

back.

late, too la - te. ___

Additional Lyrics

2. I walk with you, you walk with me.
   I talked to you, you talked to me.

L.A. Woman

Words and Music by The Doors

Copyright © 1971 Doors Music Co.
Copyright Renewed
All Rights Reserved   Used by Permission

keep on ris - in'. Mis - ter Mo - jo ___ ris - in'.

Mis - ter Mo - jo ris - in'.

Mo - jo ris - in'. Mis - ter Mo - jo ris - in'.

Mis - ter Mo - jo ris - in'. Got to

keep on ris - in'. Ris - in', ris - in'.

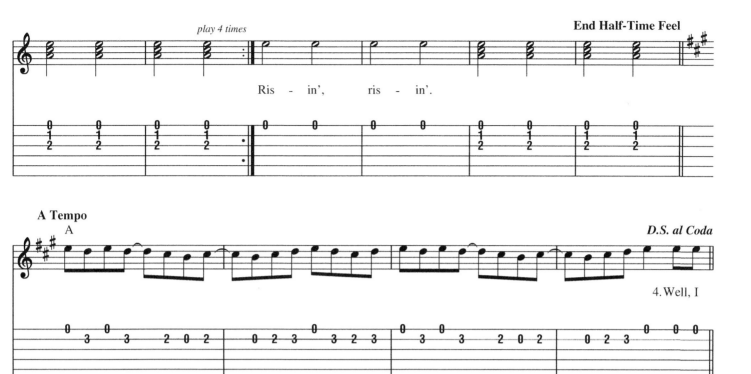

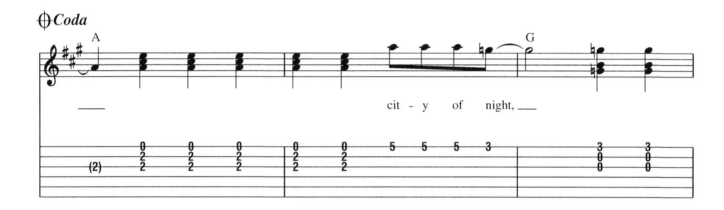

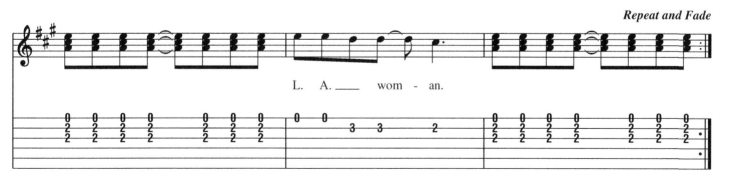

Light My Fire

Words and Music by The Doors

G   D   F   B♭   E♭   A♭

A   Am7   F♯m7   B   E   C

Strum Pattern: 1, 6
Pick Pattern: 2, 6

Intro
Moderate Rock

G   D   F   B♭   E♭   A♭

Verse

1. You know that it would be un-true. ___ You
2. *See Additional Lyrics*

know that I would be a liar. ___ If I was to say to you, ___

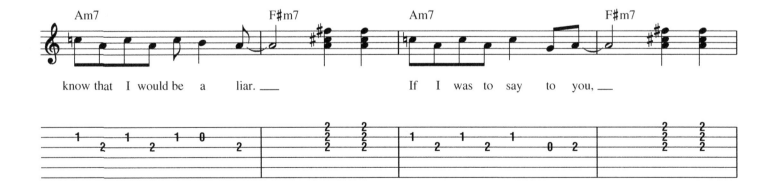

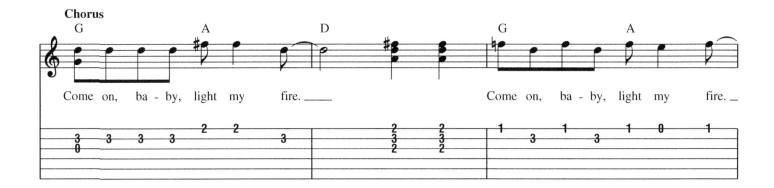

Chorus

Come on, ba - by, light my fire. ____ Come on, ba - by, light my fire. __

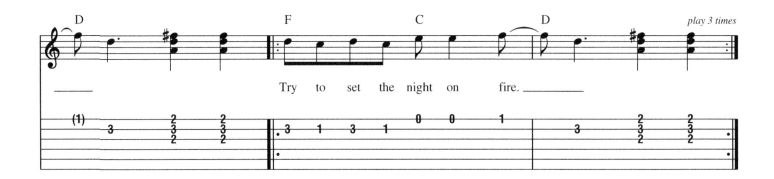

Try to set the night on fire. _____

play 3 times

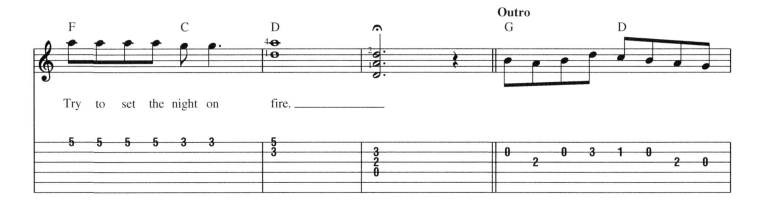

Outro

Try to set the night on fire. _____

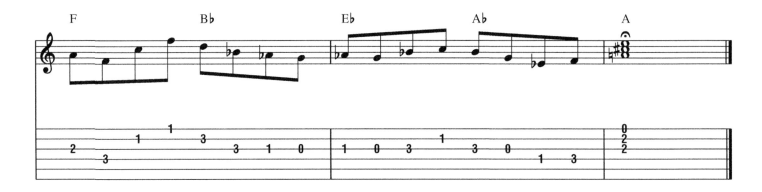

Additional Lyrics

2. The time to hesitate is through,
No time to wallow in the mire.
Try now we can only lose,
And our love become a funeral pyre.

Love Street

Words and Music by The Doors

Strum Pattern: 4, 5
Pick Pattern: 4, 5

Verse
Moderately

she has mon - keys,   la - zy dia - mond - stud - ded flun - kies.

Chorus

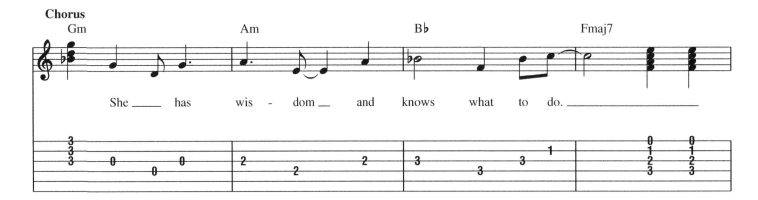

She ___ has wis - dom ___ and knows what to do. ___

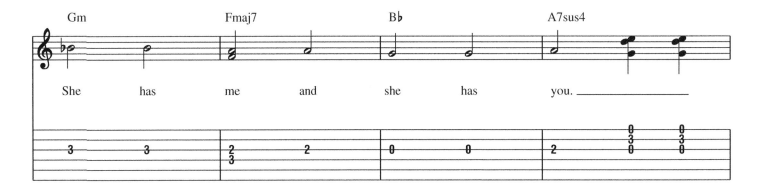

She has me and she has you. ___

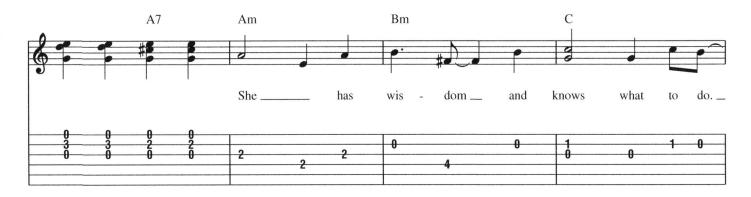

She ___ has wis - dom ___ and knows what to do. ___

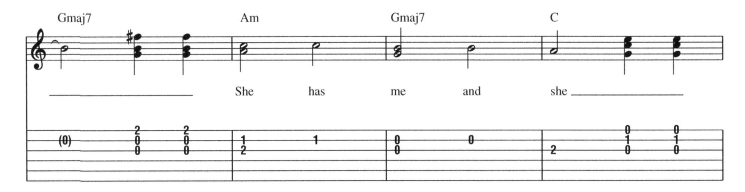

___ She has me and she ___

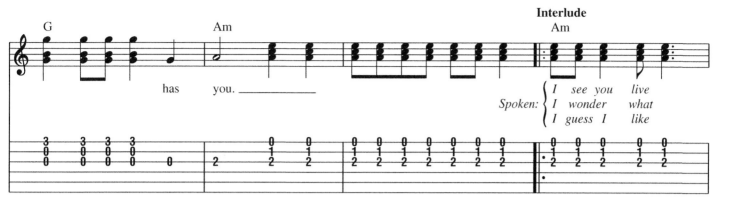

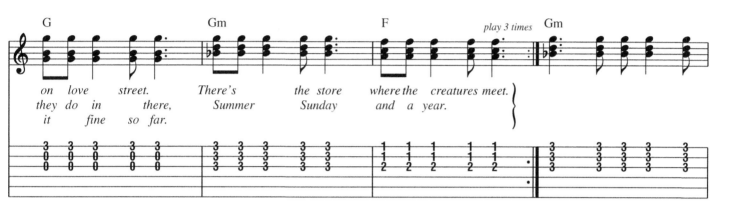

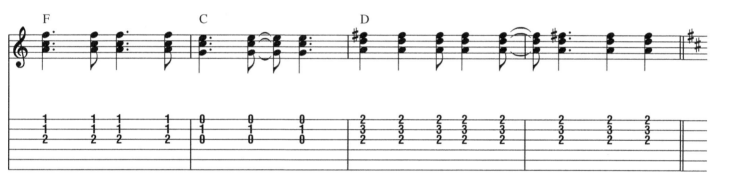

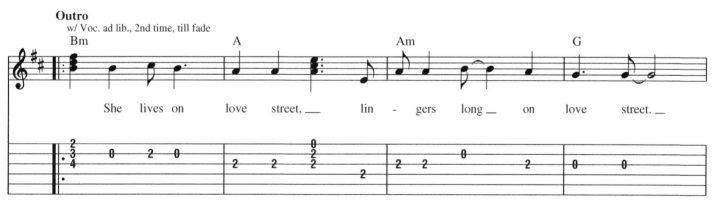

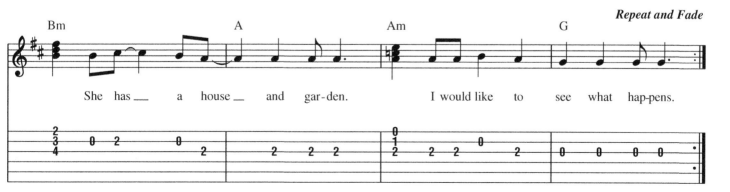

Love Her Madly

Words and Music by The Doors

Don't you love her ___ face? ___ Don't you love her as ___ she's

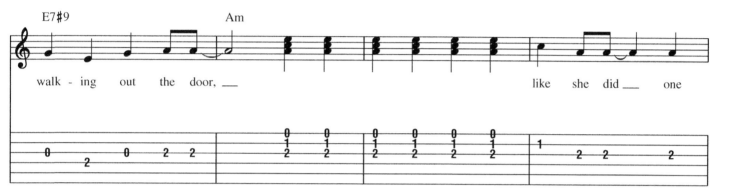

walk - ing out the door, ___ like she did ___ one

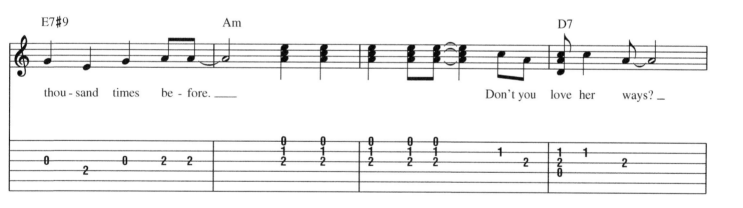

thou - sand times be - fore. ___ Don't you love her ways? ___

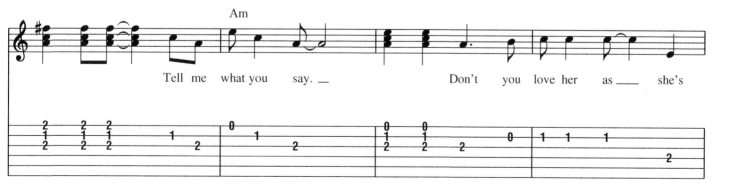

Tell me what you say. ___ Don't you love her as ___ she's

walk - ing out ___ the door? ___

Chorus

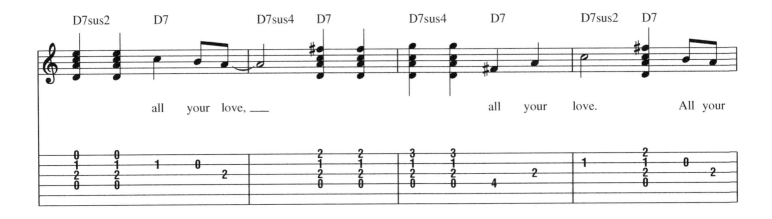

All your love, ___ all your love, ___

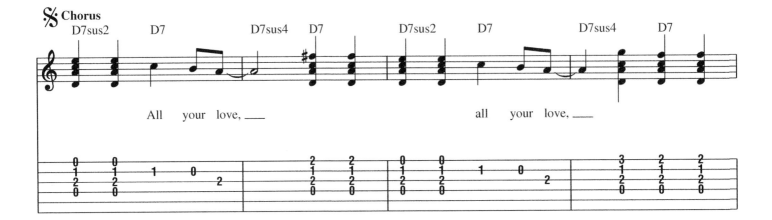

all your love, ___ all your love. All your

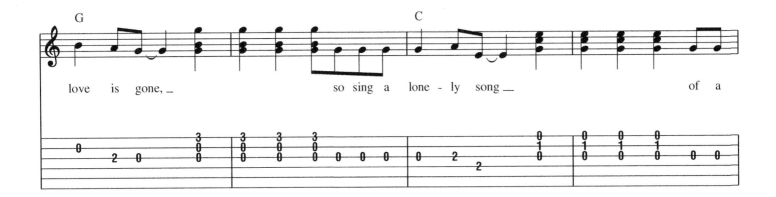

love is gone, _ so sing a lone - ly song _ of a

Love Me Two Times

Words and Music by The Doors

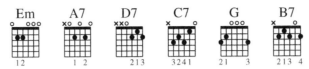

Strum Pattern: 1, 3
Pick Pattern: 2, 3

1. Love me two times, ba - by. Love me twice to - day.
2. *See Additional Lyrics*

Love me two times, girl, I'm goin' a - way.

Love me two times, girl, one for to - mor-row, one just for to - day.

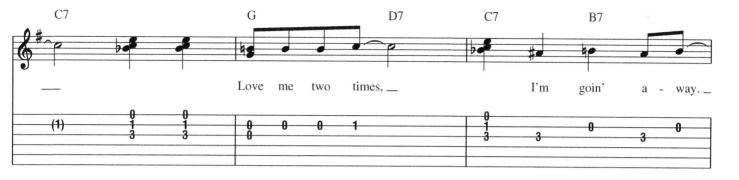

Love me two times, __ I'm goin' a - way. __

1.

2.

Outro

Love me two times, __ I'm goin' a - way. __

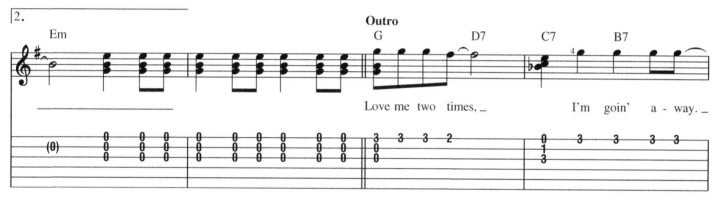

Love me two times, __

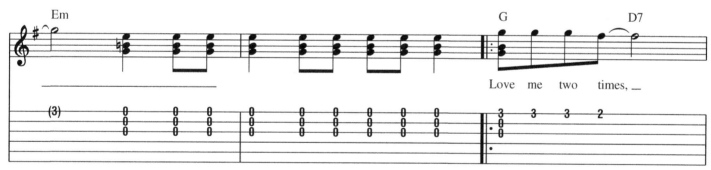

1., 2., 3.

4.

I'm goin' a - way. _____

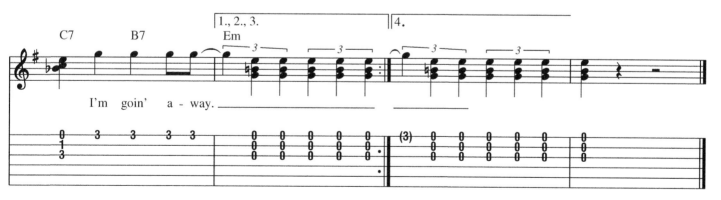

Additional Lyrics

2. Love me one time, could not speak.
Love me one time, yeah, my knees got weak.
Love me two times, girl, last me all through the week.
Love me two times, I'm goin' away.

People Are Strange

Words and Music by The Doors

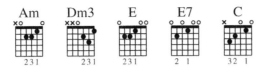

Strum Pattern: 1, 4
Pick Pattern: 1, 2

Verse
Moderately

1., 2., 3. Peo - ple are strange _ when you're a stran - ger, fa - ces look ug - ly

when you're a - lone. _ Wom - en seem wick - ed when you're un - want - ed,

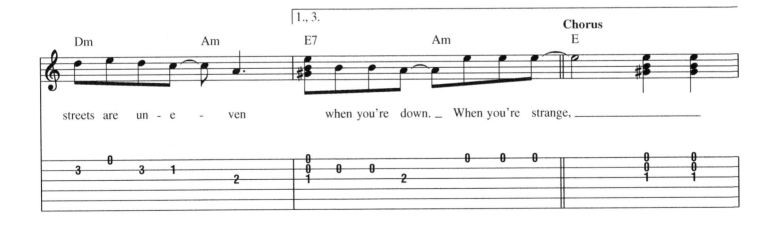

1., 3.

Chorus

streets are un - e - ven when you're down. _ When you're strange, _____

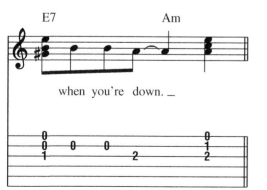

Riders on the Storm

Words and Music by The Doors

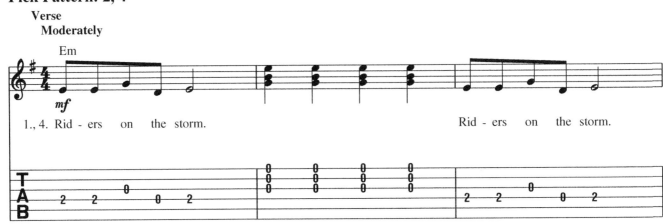

Strum Pattern: 4, 6
Pick Pattern: 2, 4

Verse
Moderately

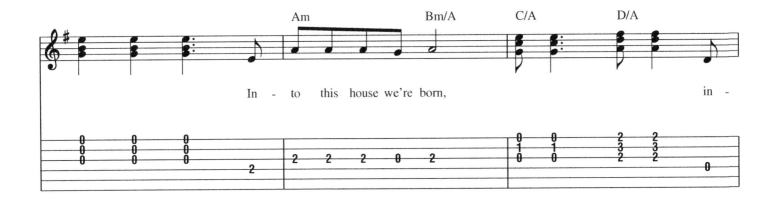

1., 4. Rid - ers on the storm. Rid - ers on the storm.

In - to this house we're born, in -

to this world we're thrown like a dog with - out a bone, an

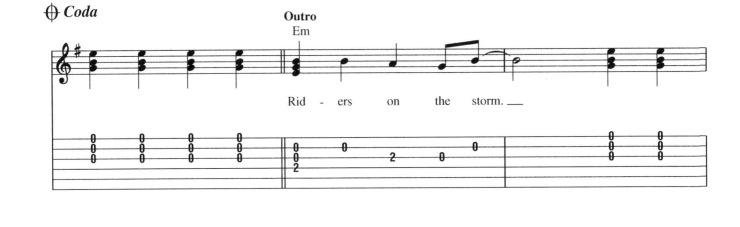

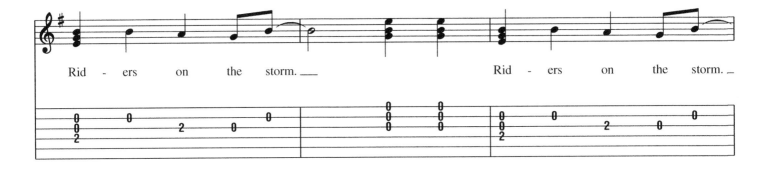

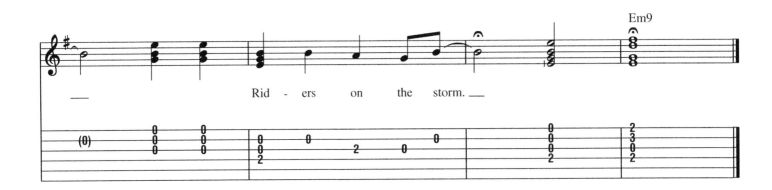

Additional Lyrics

3. Girl, you gotta love your man.
   Girl, you gotta love your man.
   Take him by the hand, make him understand.
   The world on you depends, our life will never end.
   Gotta love your man.

Soul Kitchen

Words and Music by The Doors

Strum Pattern: 4, 6
Pick Pattern: 3, 4

Verse

Moderate Rock

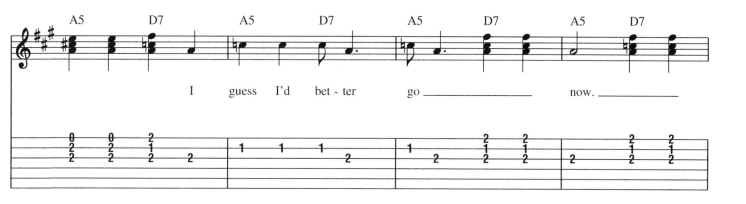

1. Well, the (4.) clock says it's time to close _____ now. _____

I guess I'd bet-ter go _____ now. _____

To Coda

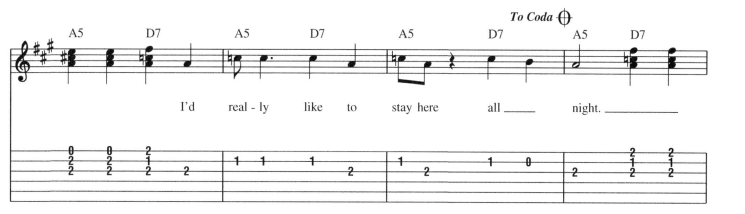

I'd real-ly like to stay here all ____ night. _____

Roadhouse Blues

Words and Music by The Doors

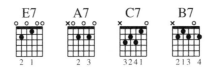

E7   A7   C7   B7

Strum Pattern: 1, 3
Pick Pattern: 1, 3

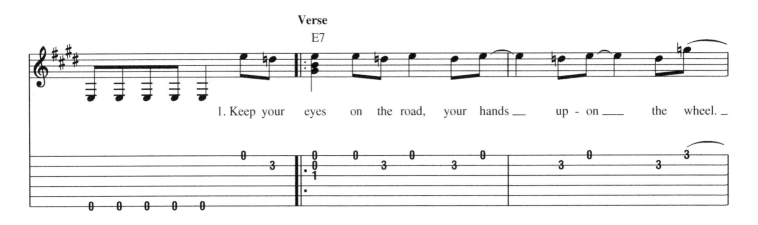

go - in' to the road - house, gon - na have a real, ____ a, good time.__

Verse

E7

2. Yeah, in back of the road - house they
4. *See Additional Lyrics*

1.

got some bun - ga - lows. ___ Yeah, in

2.

And that's for the peo - ple who like to go ___ down

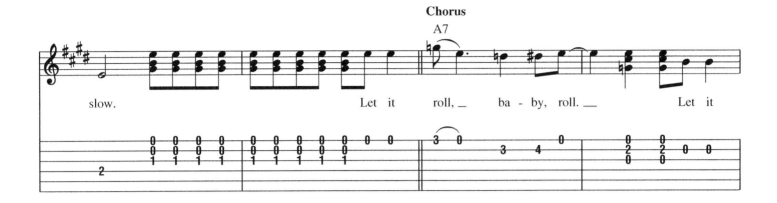

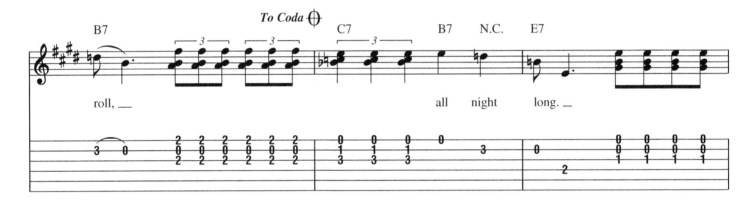

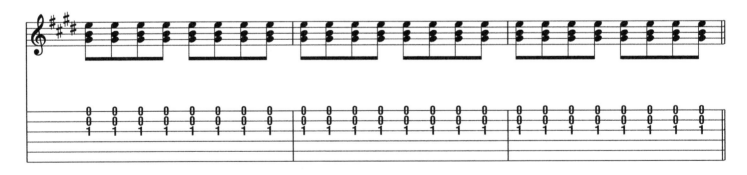

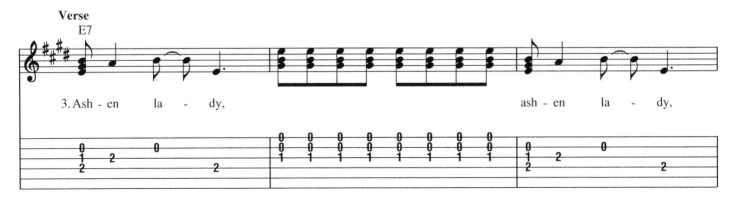

Additional Lyrics

4. When I woke up this mornin' I got myself a beer.
When I woke up this mornin' I got myself a beer.
The future's uncertain and the end is always near.

Strange Days

Words and Music by The Doors

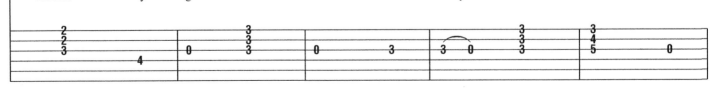

Em   Am   F#   Gm   Cm   G   B   Bb   F   E

Strum Pattern: 4, 6
Pick Pattern: 2, 6

Intro
Moderate Rock

play 4 times

Em

mf

Verse

Em   Am   Em

1. Strange ___ days have found us. ___
2., 3. *See Additional Lyrics*

Am   Em   Am   Em   F#

Strange ___ days have tracked us down. ___

Gm   Cm   Gm   Cm

They're goin' ___ to de - stroy ___ our

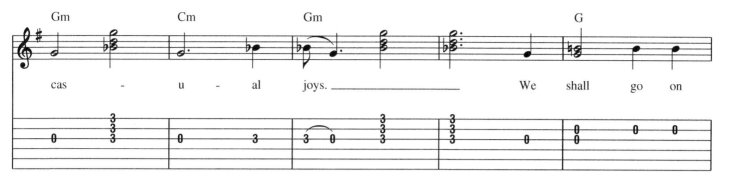

cas - u - al joys. _____ We shall go on

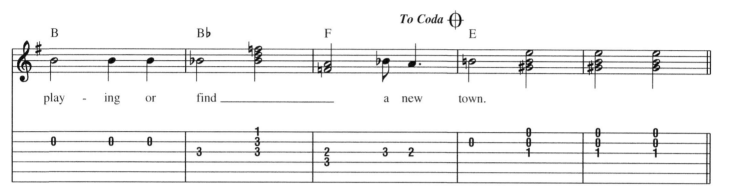

To Coda ⊕

play - ing or find _____ a new town.

Interlude

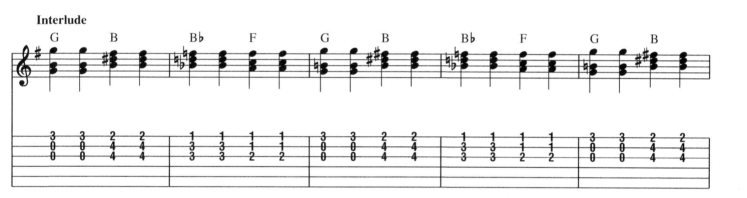

⊕ *Coda*

2nd time, D.S. al Coda

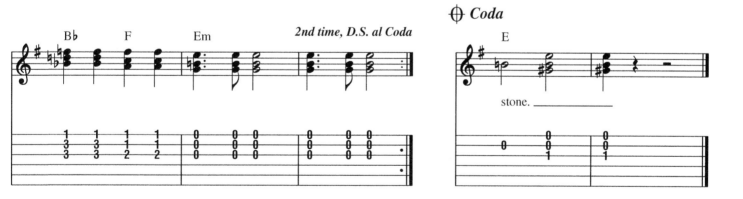

stone. _____

Additional Lyrics

2. Strange eyes fill strange rooms.
   Voices will signal their tired end.
   The hostess is grinning, her guests sleep from sinning.
   Hear me talk of sin and you know this is it.

3. Strange days have found us.
   And through their strange hours
   We linger alone; bodies confused, memories misused.
   As we run from the day to a strange night of stone.

Summer's Almost Gone

Words and Music by The Doors

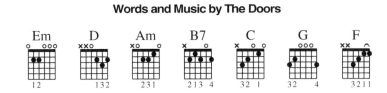

Strum Pattern: 2, 3
Pick Pattern: 2, 3

Chorus
Moderately

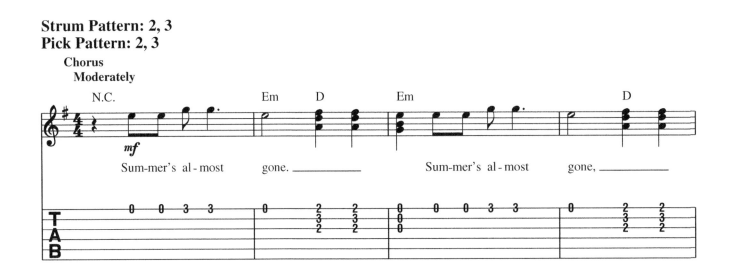

Sum-mer's al-most gone. _____ Sum-mer's al-most gone, _____

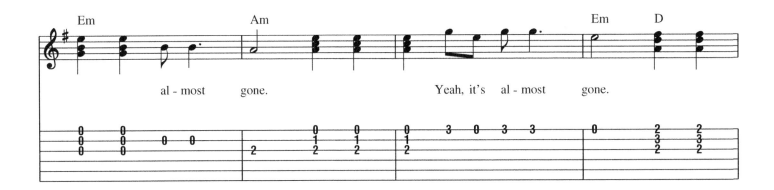

al-most gone. Yeah, it's al-most gone.

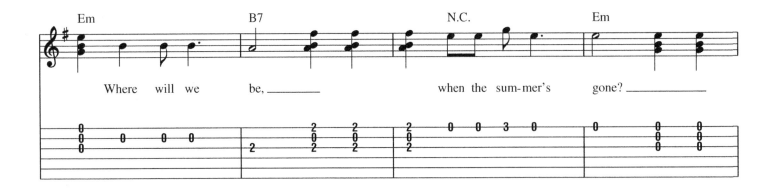

Where will we be, _____ when the sum-mer's gone? _____

Verse

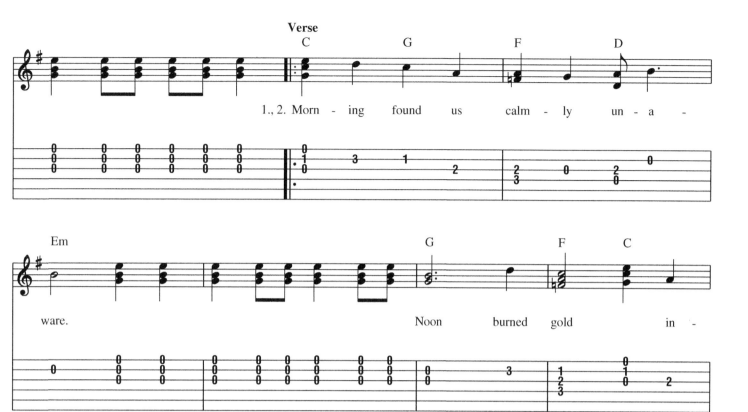

1., 2. Morn - ing found us calm - ly un - a -

ware. Noon burned gold in -

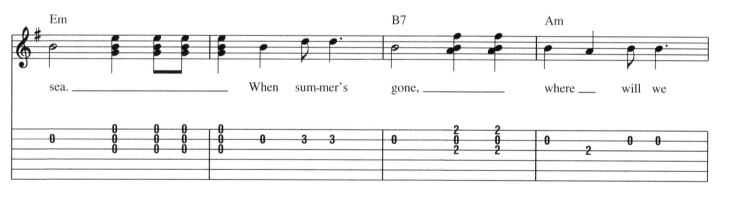

to our hair. At night we swam the laugh-ing

sea. _____ When sum-mer's gone, _____ where ___ will we

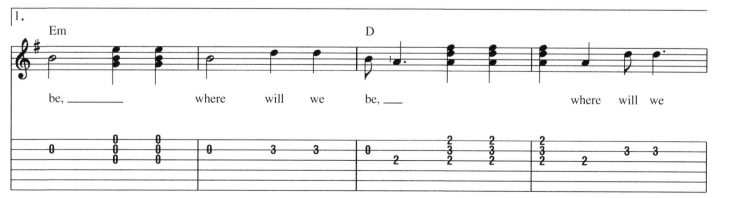

be, _____ where will we be, ___ where will we

Touch Me

Words and Music by The Doors

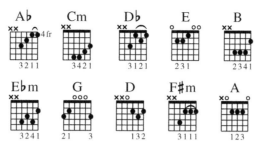

Strum Pattern: 4, 5
Pick Pattern: 1, 5

Intro
Moderately Fast

1., 2. C'-mon, ___ c'-mon, c'-mon, c'-mon now

Verse

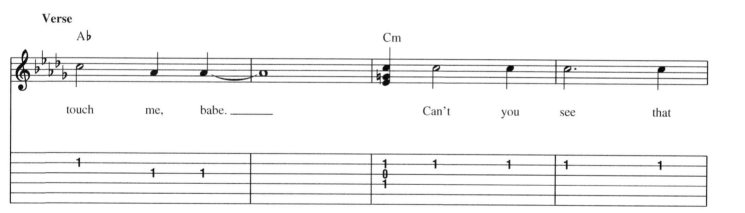

touch me, babe. ___ Can't you see that

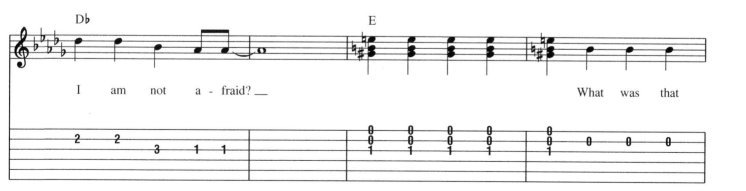

I am not a-fraid? ___ What was that

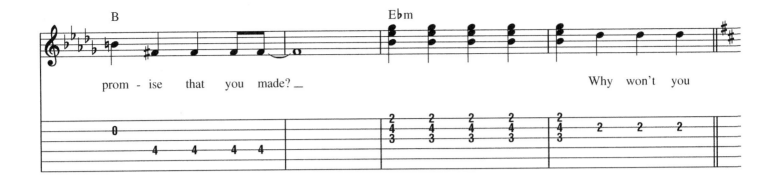

prom - ise that you made? __ Why won't you

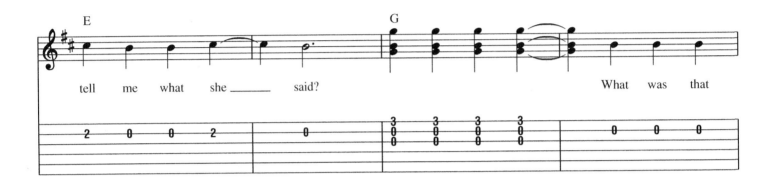

tell me what she _____ said? What was that

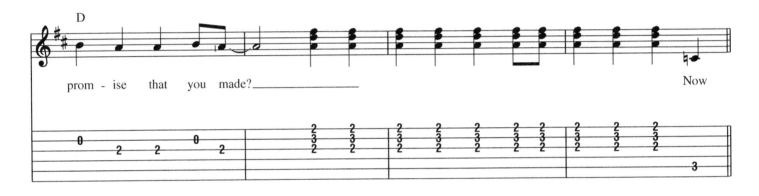

prom - ise that you made? _____ Now

Chorus

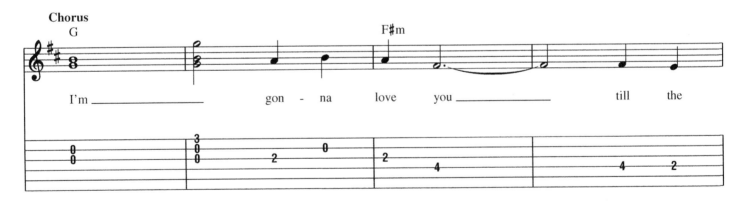

I'm _____ gon - na love you _____ till the

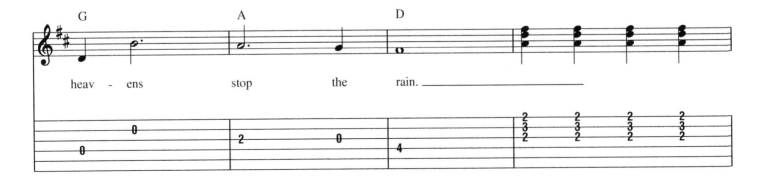

heav - ens stop the rain. _____

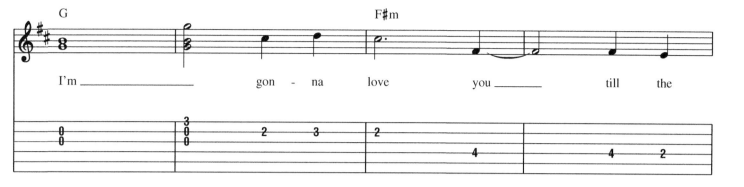

I'm _____ gon - na love you _____ till the

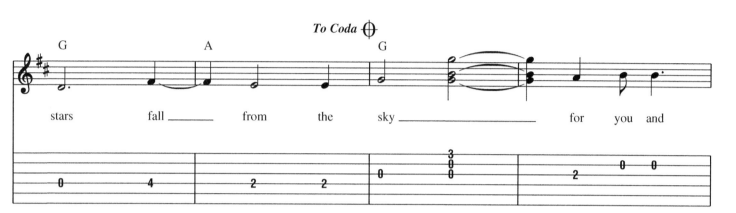

stars fall _____ from the sky _____ for you and

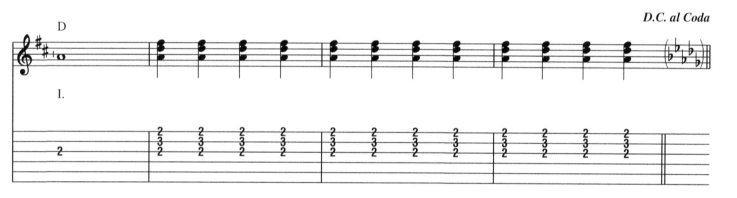

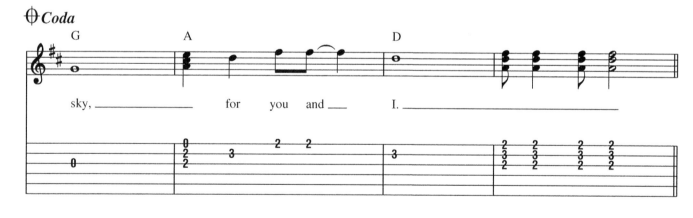

Twentieth Century Fox

Words and Music by The Doors

Chorus

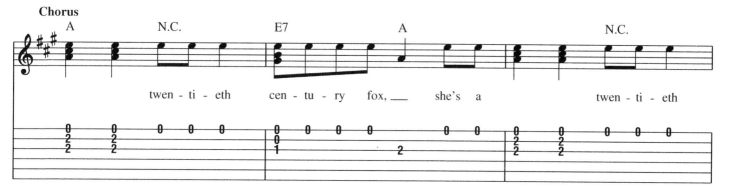

twen - ti - eth cen - tu - ry fox, ___ she's a twen - ti - eth

cen - tu - ry fox. ___

No tears, ___ no fears, ___ no
Got the world ___ locked up ___ in -

To Coda ⊕

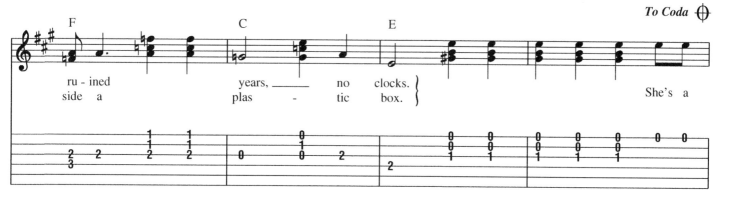

ru - ined years, ___ no clocks.
side a plas - tic box.

She's a

Interlude

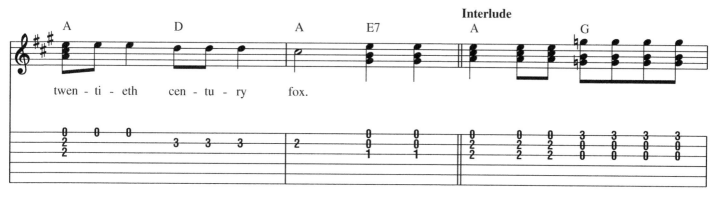

twen - ti - eth cen - tu - ry fox.

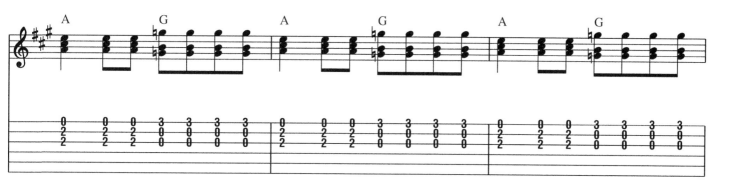

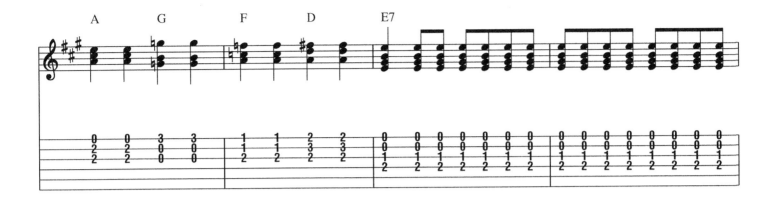

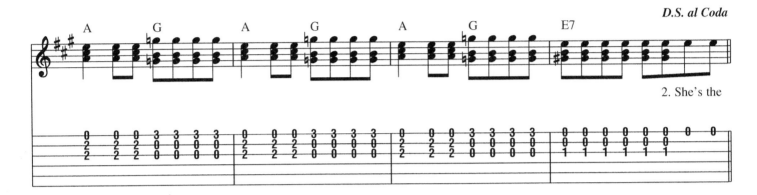

Additional Lyrics

2. She's the queen of cool, and she's the lady who waits.
Since her mind left school, it never hesitates.
She won't waste time on element'ry talk.

Waiting for the Sun

Words and Music by The Doors

Strum Pattern: 4, 6
Pick Pattern: 3, 5

Intro
Moderately

1. At

Verse

first flash of E - den we raced down to the sea,
2., 3. *See Additional Lyrics*

stand - ing there on free - dom's shore.

Wait - ing for the sun, wait - ing for the sun,

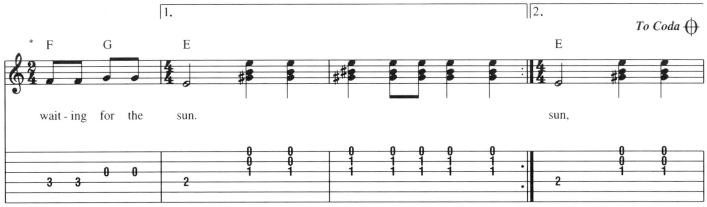

wait - ing   for   the   sun.   sun,

* Use Pattern 10

Bridge

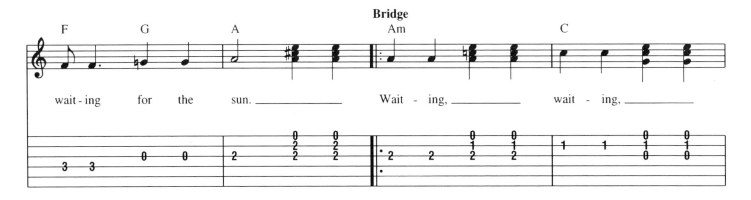

wait - ing   for   the   sun. _____   Wait - ing, _____   wait - ing, _____

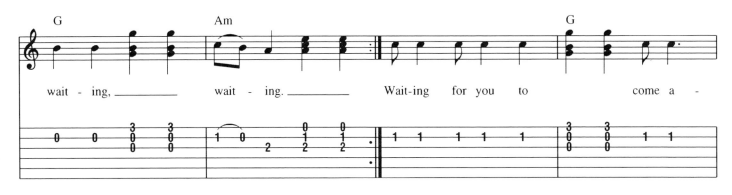

wait - ing, _____   wait - ing. _____   Wait-ing   for   you   to   come a -

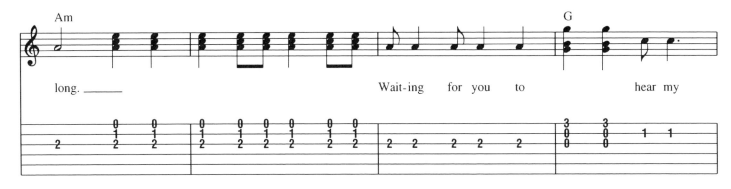

long. _____   Wait-ing   for   you   to   hear my

song. _____   Wait-ing   for   you   to   come a - long. _

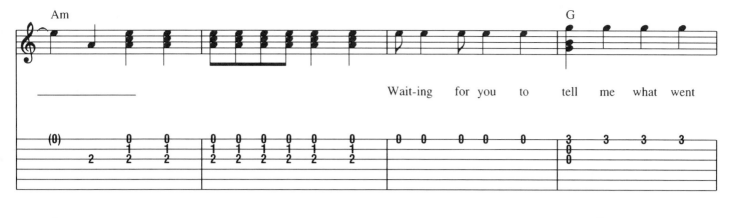

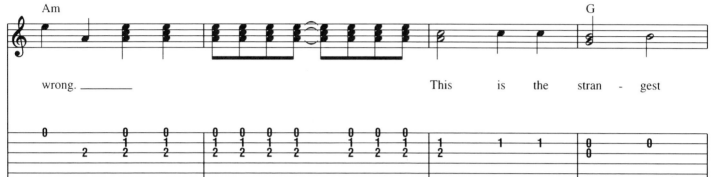

D.S. al Coda
(take 2nd ending)

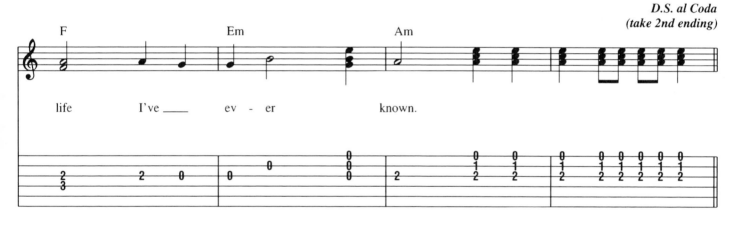

 Coda

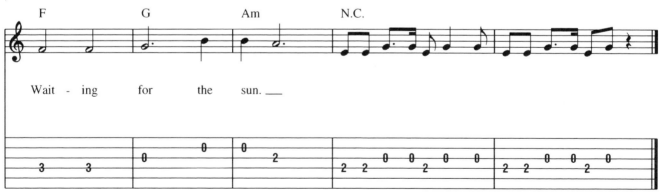

Additional Lyrics

2., 3. Can't you feel it, now that spring has come;
That it's time to live in the scattered sun.
Waiting for the sun, waiting for the sun,
Waiting for the sun.